Take Charge of Your Brand

Quick and simple techniques to help you own and manage your personal brand for professional and personal success

GUISSELLE NUÑEZ

DEDICATION

This book is dedicated to my parents, Donald and Sonia, my brother, Alexander, and close friends, especially my ya-ya's, who on a daily basis, during our "morning commute conference calls," have animated discussions related to our personal and professional lives and provide each other with constant and unconditional intellectual and emotional support. Additionally, I'm blessed to have my husband, Ron, as my best-friend, my cheerleader, and power partner...without him, my purpose and passion for personal branding may not have been born.

And I can't forget our family dog, Murphy, our pitbull. Frequent experiences with prejudice against his breed, inspired me to start a personal branding campaign, to convince one person at a time, that his (dog breed) brand is not one of a vicious dog, but instead, his brand is of the nanny dog, loving, friendly and playful.

@murphypittiewithpurpose

CONTENTS

ACKNOWLEDGMENTS

Thank you Tesa Colvin, who in addition to being my
Publishing Coach & Consultant, was my book writing cheerleader. If you
want to write a book, visit her website, www.borrowmymba.com

Sheryl Sandberg, Author of "Lean In," a book that inspired me to
understand and be more aware of the gender and cultural barriers that may
hinder my professional and personal growth. This awareness allowed me to
take charge of my brand.

INTRODUCTION
Take charge of your brand, OR be branded by others

They say you teach, what you want to learn; and every time I teach a personal branding workshop, and even as I wrote this book, my passion and curiosity only increased to continue my lifelong learning of personal branding; how to develop and communicate your value to the world, and how to manage it. This passion, knowledge and experience is what I want to share with each of you.

Important Note: The first part of the book provides you with a high-level overview of personal branding , and strategies to learn how to manage it. *Ideally, this book is for people <u>who are ready</u> to begin the journey of taking charge of their personal brand, invest the time to manage it, and are ready to reach their professional and personal goals.* The strategies I lay out for you to follow, are not panaceas. I encourage you to tailor the strategies and tactics to your style, and most importantly, understand that managing your personal brand takes time, courage, focus, and patience. This book will provide you with a roadmap to start to manage or improve the management of your personal brand. The second part of the book, the workbook, provide you the activities to help you dive in and start to think about and implement the branding strategies outlined in this book.

What is a personal brand?
You already have a personal brand whether you buy into this thinking or not. Your personal brand is a combination of your image and

reputation. How you present and conduct yourself daily forms the foundation for your brand. Others impact your personal brand too, through their communication and actions.

Why is a personal brand important to you?

Success in your career requires you to be intimately aware of how you are presenting yourself to others. Whether you realize this, or not, you already have a personal brand that defines and illustrates you to the wider world, who you are, where you have been, and where you are going.

A strong personal brand allows you to determine and communicate who you are, what makes you great, what separates you from your peers, and what's valuable to those who are making decisions about you. All of your social media followers are not going to help you build your brand if you are not able to communicate your value to them consistently, credibly, and authentically. Your colleagues or manager may not invite you on project teams if they don't know who you are, your strengths and what you bring to the table that's of value to them.

Think of your personal brand as a way to take control of your reputation and creating a (personal branding) statement that summarizes who you are. Below are three reasons you should care about taking charge of your personal brand:

1) *Define what you stand for:* owning your personal brand reveals to the world who you are, what you believe in, and what you stand for. Knowing these things, and being able to communicate them, should be liberating, because your brand is ultimately who YOU have chosen to become. This is part of learning how to differentiate yourself.

2) *Differentiate yourself from the competition:* in a crowded marketplace, every company has to work on making sure their (brand) product is the one you will choose to purchase. Well, you are a product also. If you want to get ahead in your career, be invited to participate on project teams, or establish yourself as an expert in your field, you need to stand out from the rest of your competition. How do you do that? You build a personal branding strategy that will help you learn how to communicate your value, experience, and aspirations to others.

3) *Explain how your past fits into your present:* As your career(s) change, so does your brand. Your career will indelibly change, and with that change, you will grow in different ways. Owning your personal brand allows you to pull professional (and personal) experiences

together and explain your evolution by developing your narrative. You own your narrative, so this is your chance to reinvent yourself and tell your story.

Additionally, owning and communicating your personal brand can also help you attract new clients, employees or employers. In 1983, Steve Jobs was able to recruit the President of Pepsi, John Sculley to join the Apple team, by convincing him that Apple wasn't just selling computers. Sculley believed that Steve Jobs was going to change the world. Jobs asked Sculley, "Do you want to sell sugar water for the rest of your life? Or do you want to come with me and change the world?"

If you define what you stand for, can differentiate yourself, and explain how your past fits with your present (and future)…and learn how to communicate that narrative to the world—you can also change the world! What is in your heart and soul? What do you really care about? What are your passions? Turn those ideas and beliefs into content you can share with the world. Write a blog. Build an online community of followers. Launch a YouTube channel. Become a professional speaker. The list goes on…

But, remember, your brand can't be manufactured. You need to build an authentic and credible personal brand, otherwise people will smell fake a mile away. Your personal brand and how you communicate it to the world must reflect your beliefs.

Do you think you have a credible personal brand? Ask yourself these questions:

- Do people have a clear understanding of what you do and the value you bring?
- What words, concepts, and ideas do people associate with your name and image?

If it takes you more than a few minutes to answer these questions, then I would recommend you build a personal branding strategy for yourself. So keep reading…and I'll show you how…

How do you create and manage your personal brand?

How do you take control of your brand, allowing you to influence and shape what you would like people to say and think about you? This is done through personal branding. Personal branding is an intentional process of developing a strategy and actions to guide your brand. This book and its accompanying workbook will outline a strategy so that you can have the tools and material you need to begin developing and managing your personal brand.

Personal branding is not about likeability...it's about authenticity. In the most simple terms, I define authenticity to be as being consistent in word and action, having the same fundamental character in different roles, and being comfortable with your past. Laura Vanderkam, in her article "What does Authenticity really mean?" says that to be "authentic also requires some skillfulness especially in a work environment. For example, you need to think about how the person inside of you comes across. In your personal life, you may love to share your religious faith because it's what motivates you and inspires you. That doesn't mean you should proselytize in staff meetings." [IV] So there needs to be a balance between being yourself, but also being cognizant of how others may perceive you.

Personal branding is a purposeful journey you choose to take and manage in order to help you communicate to the world the most authentic you. In this book and workbook, I lay out three ways you can start to own and subsequently manage your personal brand. These include the following strategies:

PLANNING: Know what you want. Know where to get it.
ASSESSMENT: Know who you are.
EXPRESSION: Know, how and who you will share with.

The proceeding chapters and workbook will touch on each strategy, and provide you with guiding questions that will take you through the process of being able to learn how to communicate who you are, what you stand for and how to differentiate yourself. In other words, having a personal branding strategy will be able to help you determine your branding goals, assess your brand, and learn how to promote your brand. The workbook provides you with easy to follow templates and questions. Each section builds on the last, so that your end product will be the development of your personal branding statement. This statement will be your new narrative of your brand story.

Personal Branding...a very personal topic for me...

My story starts as a 25 year-old, taking a risk on love. It sounds pretty simple, but my risk had complications. The person I fell in love with, was the mayor for the city of San Jose. He was 23 years my senior, newly separated, and you can imagine that made for a tantalizing media story, frenzy and lots of gossip! In any case, my risk on love paid off, but in return, I was thrust into a very public life, which left me with the huge task of fighting the stigma of how my husband and I began our relationship.

So, I knew I had to build my own identity, and my tasks included—dealing with that stigma, coming out of the shadow of my husband's position and building a career for myself *(it's not easy finding a job that won't result in conflicts of interest, or perceptions of conflict of interest, with City Hall)*, and between all of that, figuring out how to be a constant and supportive partner, through all of the challenges that elected office may bring to an individual and a family.

I didn't have anybody to help me lay out a personal branding plan, nor was this subject as popular as it is now, so self-help resources materials were limited.

Essentially through instinct, being authentic, positivity, and research, I started the journey and found my passion for the field of marketing. My desire to help organizations find their value and help them communicate that to the world, blended into passions for marketing and personal branding. What could have been a very dark and negative personal experience, turned out to be a light in my life. Helping others find their voice and teaching them how to communicate their value has become a purpose for my brand and my life, which in turn, has allowed me to learn how to communicate my own brand to the world.

What's next?

> *A personal brand is "comprised of your character, competence and charisma. It's who you are, what you do, and why you're special. You have to create it, claim it, then make sure everyone in your network knows about it." (Tom Peters)*

Personal branding is not just for CEOs, someone who has political aspirations, famous entertainers, or recent college graduates. Personal branding is something that touches all of us, at all stages in our personal and professional lives and careers, and whether you know it or not, you are branding yourself every day. The question is—do you know what your brand represents to others? Do you "package" your brand in such a way that it represents your goals, aspirations and purpose? How do you weave brand management into your everyday life?

This book and workbook is intended to provide you with a *simple* way to build your own pathway and strategy to determine your branding goals, assess your brand, and learn how to promote your brand. The personal branding strategies laid out in this book are from my personal journey, my research, my hands-on experience in helping others communicate and develop their value and brand, and I too practice these strategies on a daily basis. *(I really do...and if you are serious about managing your brand, you will need to do the same thing also—find time (15-20 minutes per day) on a daily basis to manage your brand—more about this in later chapters).* Your brand is working 24 hours a day; make sure it is communicating what you want. **What have you done for your brand today?**

1 - PERSONAL BRANDING - THE BASICS

"All of us need to understand the importance of branding. We are CEOs of our own companies: Me Inc. To be in business today, our most important job is to be head marketer for the brand called You."
— Tom Peters in Fast Company

Build your personal brand first, in order to build your career. Personal branding is a vital part of building your career. It can have long-term effects on your career path as well as your earning potential. I hope by the time you finish reading this book you understand why I emphasize the importance of owning your brand. Before you can build your own personal brand, you must understand what it is and how to wield it to your benefit for professional and personal growth.

What's your favorite brand?

Think of your favorite brand or brands. What are they? Describe them in one to three words. Do they evoke an image or a feeling? When I pose this question to my participants at my personal branding workshops, some common responses include Apple (modern design, functional), Volvo (safe), BMW (fast), Nordstrom (customer service focused), Oprah Winfrey (inspirational or authenticity), Steve Jobs (for innovation, pursuit of excellence), Martha Stewart (for domesticity), Zappos (stands for internet shoes), and Google (stands for search). Speaking of which, Stewart, is an excellent example of someone who was able to maintain her brand even during and after her prison sentence.. Ever wonder how she did that? We will have an in depth discussion on reinventing and rebranding yourself in later chapters.

Can you acknowledge that you are also a brand? Whether you realize it or not, your colleagues and friends are right now, using specific adjectives to describe YOU. Do you have any idea which adjectives are used to describe you? Would you agree with other people's description of YOU and your strengths? Upcoming, we will discuss (and give you an example) an assessment survey that you can conduct on your own to confirm whether your friends and colleagues describe YOU as you'd want to be described.

But for now, let's continue with our quick introduction about personal branding…

Personal Branding—what is it?

Tom Peters, considered to be the godfather of personal branding, defines personal branding as, "comprised of your character, competence and charisma. It's who you are, what you do, and why you're special. You have to create it, claim it, and then make sure everyone in your network knows about it." (Considered to be the first content written on personal branding, I recommend you read the article in *Fast Company*, "The Brand Called You," by Tom Peters, 1997).[1]

And…if I may be so bold as to add to the godfather's great definition of personal branding—I would also say that personal branding is:

- What you want to be known for in the minds of others
- It goes beyond popularity, and it's not about impressing people with what you can do, you need to have substance to back up who you say you are and the value you bring *(so you can't fake it, and don't oversell, people will eventually find out the truth!)*
- Something you manage on a daily basis, not something that just happens
- It's a *continual process*…as you grow, so does your brand… *(not to be morbid---but---when you die…your brand still remains in the minds of people who knew you, or those that hear about you from those who knew you!)*

Tom Peters says we have to become the "CEOs of ME, Inc." So if that's the case—then, can you start by identifying the qualities or characteristics that make you distinctive from your competitors or your colleagues? What have you done lately — this week — to make yourself stand out? What would your colleagues say is your greatest and clearest strength? Your most noteworthy (as in, worthy of note) personal trait?

Become Your Own Brand Manager

Now, let's be realistic, answering the questions posed above, and building your brand is not going to happen overnight. You need to become a brand manager for YOU (YOU- the brand). This is why this work, is a continual process, and something you manage every day!

So now that we have established your new role, as brand manager, in this company called YOU, then what's the marketing strategy we are going to roll out for the product called YOU?

I recommend you <u>break your personal brand management strategy into three sections, Planning, Assessment and Expression</u>. We will have an opportunity to review these three personal brand management strategies in Chapter Three and in the workbook. For now—here's a quick introduction:

1. PLANNING: Know what you want. Know where to get it.
- **What are your goals for branding YOU?** These could include but are not limited to: Visibility; Preference; Credibility; Engagement; Influence; Perception.
- **Who is your audience and who do you want to influence?** Choosing a niche or target market will make personal branding easier.

2. ASSESSMENT: Know who you are. Are you on track to reach your planning goals?
- **What is your brand identity as it stands now?** Identifying "BRAND YOU" involves looking at yourself and your attributes in a brutally honest way. Feeling good about yourself and your current place in life will lead to increased confidence which will make the act of branding yourself a more natural activity.
- Ask those close to you: "what words would you use to describe me?"

What do you want to be known for?

3. EXPRESSION: Know how, and who, you will share "BRAND YOU" with.

- **How do you reach the people you want to influence? Develop a plan.** There are many options of how you can express your personal brand, and we will cover more examples in Chapter 3 and in the workbook.

Overall you need to be positive. Don't be fake, be yourself and show your passion! Your brand needs to be authentic, needs to have integrity, and purpose.

Personal Brand Spotlight:

Tom Clancy, best-selling author of dozens of thrillers, 100 million books sold, including creating a famed series starring Jack Ryan, died in 2013. Tom Clancy was known for his "technology, military tactics or geo-political maneuvering" [II] thrillers like 'The Hunt for Red October' which was turned into a box-office hit movie. Tom Clancy is a great example of two things—one, how your brand lives on even after you die. Two, the re-invention of your brand.

Tom Clancy's name lives on, and it's no longer the name of a man, it's a brand.[III] A brand that signals the undercover world of spies and counter-terrorism, and a certain kind of taut military thriller. A gaming company, Ubisoft bought the rights to the name "Tom Clancy" and they sell videogames that represent Tom Clancy's style of military tactics and action. Several authors have continued to write stories based on Clancy's characters, like Jack Ryan. It's notable that the writers' own names appear in small type on the covers, while the brand name "Tom Clancy" fills nearly half of the page.

But before Tom Clancy became a household name he was an insurance salesman. His passion was to become a writer and so he wrote on the weekends and his spare time. At 37 years of age, "The Hunt for Red October" was released to great acclaim and phenomenal success –he had hoped it would sell 5,000 copies, but it ended up selling well over two million copies. Tom Clancy reinvented himself just by writing a novel.

Reinventing yourself is possible, but you need to be ready to do the work, craft a strategy, and develop a continuous lifelong regime of managing your brand.

2 - MANAGING THE BRAND ELEMENTS OF THE BRAND 'YOU'

"Be Yourself, Everyone Else is Already Taken."
-Oscar Wilde

How does a product brand relate to me?
Philip Kotler is considered the father of modern marketing. That bit of trivia is for you marketing enthusiasts out there—of which I am definitely one! By the way, for those of you who are interested in the topic, Kotler authored superb books on marketing management. I use them constantly in my marketing classes and recommend them highly. There are many workable definitions of a brand— but, I consider Kotler's definition, which follows below, to be the best:

> *A brand is a name, term, sign, symbol or design, combination of them, intended to identify the goods or services of one seller or group of sellers and to differentiate them from those of competitors.*

So how does that definition of a product brand relate to you?

Since we agree that YOU are a brand, then, you need to figure out how to distinguish yourself from your competition. YOU are always in competition—for jobs, promotions, joining or obtaining invitations to project teams, special assignments, and much more! People are buying, and you are on the shelf competing with many other brands for their attention. Who will the buyer choose?

3

What's the purpose of a brand?

Picture yourself at a grocery store buying detergent. You are trying to choose between brands. Which do you choose? Why? Now think of YOUR brand as that product on the shelf. Why should that buyer choose you over someone else? How do you distinguish yourself from the competition surrounding you on that shelf? How have you communicated to the buyer, that what you offer is better than your competition's offer? *A strong personal brand provides the buyer with a shortcut in their decision-making.*

Our brand elements

The definition of a brand also says that it's a name, term, sign, symbol that helps identify and differentiate the product. Think of your favorite brands. How do they package themselves so that they appeal to you when they are on the shelf? This is a multi- layered decision process with many factors that contribute to our purchase decision. We don't buy products based on singular elements such as sleek packaging or the product slogan. Well, some of us do buy products for that reason, but if the product doesn't do what it's supposed to do, then you will probably think twice about purchasing that product again. So it's sleekness in packaging or catchy slogan name, may not be enough for you to purchase the product again.

A good product, and one that will be purchased over and over again, will have a number of brand elements that will be factors to our purchase decision. Those elements include, most of the time, a combination of the following: the product name or slogan, packaging that is attractive and visually appealing, a product that meets your expectations, and value for your money.

Likewise, with personal brands, we also have brand elements that motivate others with their decision to work with or promote us. These brand elements represent and form the way you package and promote yoursef to the world.

At its core, and probably most important of your brand elements is your brand promise. Your brand promise is who you are, your unique value offer, and how someone can benefit from working with you. Your brand promise has to be true and perform consistently. Remember that our actions speak louder than our words. The most successful brands deliver what they promise. Volvo and Subaru brands deliver safety. Apple delivers innovation and dependability. Target stores, deliver quality products at low prices.

So, how do we advertise our brand promise to induce buyers to give YOU a try? You need to build your total, product package look, feel, and design with your additional brand elements which include your core values, strengths, personality and image. The following brand elements build that fabulous package that makes up the brand YOU:

Core values—what do you believe in? What are the core values that drive who you are, what you do, don't do, etc?

Strengths— do you know what you are good at? Can you articulate, communicate and promote those strengths to the world? Can your buyers describe your strengths?

Personality—how do you make people feel around you? Do you smile, say hello, or are you a wallflower? What are your visual and physical cues to the world that say you are an interesting person, and that they should get to know you? This also reminds me of a quote by Maya Angelou, that I apply to my daily life, which says, "I've learned that people will forget what you said, people will forget what you did, but people will never forget how you made them feel." How does your personality and attitude leave a positive and lasting first impression?

Image— people...let's get real here...agree or disagree, but I believe we do judge a book by its cover...so how are your buyers judging you when they first meet you? Now, this is more than just about your attire, though I would argue that attire is a big part of building your image, this is also about the confidence and energy you exude, and impression you leave with your buyers.

An example--for those of you in hi-tech (where the work culture and environment could be very casual—shorts and t-shirts for some employees)...it stills matters how you dress. I met a young lady at a women's conference in Silicon Valley, at a roundtable discussion on personal branding. Her question was about her attire and her recent experiences of not getting hired for new job opportunities with her hi-tech employer. She was currently an administrative assistant, but wanted to move up, but she felt she wasn't taken seriously because she dressed too young for the jobs and so people only saw her age, and current role, not what she could be.

She understood this to be a barrier in her career growth, but she also felt she didn't want to dress in a way that didn't represent her personality. My advice to her, was, you don't have to betray your own sense of style and personality, but you do have to make some changes so that your intended audiences sees you as you desire them to see you. We discussed clothing stores that could fit her taste in clothes, but offered additional options to "dress up" casual wear and look a little more mature. For example---A blazer with a nice t-shirt, and nice jeans...you are still casual, but yet have just upgraded your look to be more professional and two notches higher than just wearing a sweater and jeans. So, this gets us back to first impressions..they do matter, and your fashion sense can speak louder than your words. Whatever your age is, dress for the position you want to hold.

Now that you have all of the brand elements together, we can build the package for our "Brand YOU."

Guess what!? Whether you realize it or not, you are already packaging yourself to the world using those brand elements we just discussed. But does your package represent how you want to be known in the mind of others? Does "BRAND YOU" look like you intend? If you are not managing those brand elements, then those elements are managing you.

What gets measured gets done. Managing YOU involves purposeful and strategic management on a daily basis. Remember—you are now a brand manager. The work to develop and maintain your personal brand is continous. *You need to be clear and strategic about how you package and promote the brand YOU.*

Personal Brand Spotlight:

Marissa Mayer, Yahoo's former CEO, is an example of how personal brand building can positively impact your career. She packaged her brand elements, and thus built a brand, that differentiated her from the competition. Her brand highlighted her as a successful, high-level hi-tech executive, female engineer.

Why was Marissa Mayer recruited for the position of CEO at Yahoo vs. other, prominent male executives at Google? According to Laura Ries, (in her article "Build a Brand, Not Just a Career" [v] it was because she had what most people didn't – she had a brand. "As Google's 20th employee and first woman engineer, she was a 'brand.' Marissa Mayer was the woman that made Google successful."

3- YOUR THREE PERSONAL BRAND STRATEGIES

"Brand yourself for the career you want, not the job you have."
— Dan Schawbel

BECOME YOUR OWN BRAND MANAGER

As I mentioned in **Chapter 1,** building your brand is not going to happen overnight. Building any successful brand requires deliberation and a continual, daily process. If you craft a strategy to manage your brand, you may be able to see results at different milestones in your plan. But creating and managing your personal brand requires time, commitment, and focus. When YOU are the brand, it is well worth putting time and effort to work on managing your brand. Now we're ready to roll out the *product* called YOU. What's our strategy?

Let's use our previously discussed <u>personal brand management strategies</u>: 1) Planning, 2) Assessment, 3) Expression:

PLANNING: Know what you want. Know where to get it.
ASSESSMENT: Know who you are.
EXPRESSION: Know, how and who you will share with.

THREE PERSONAL BRAND STRATEGIES
Let's take a deeper dive into each of the above strategies. For each one of these strategies, there are a number of tactics, to help you develop and implement your personal brand management strategies.

Developing these tactics and customizing them for YOU is your homework. To accomplish this, you'll need to carve out some time from your schedule on a daily basis to work on these tactics.

1)PLANNING—What are your goals for branding YOU? These could include but are not limited to: Visibility; Preference; Credibility; Engagement; Influence; Perception **Who is your audience and who do you want to influence?** Choosing a niche or target market will make personal branding easier. Define your key stakeholders, niche, influencers, peers, etc.

2)ASSESSMENT- What is your brand identity as it stands now? Identifying BRAND YOU involves looking at yourself and your attributes and weaknesses in a brutally honest way. This tactic involves assessing *your persona, your promise, and building your personal brand statement.* For more in-depth  exercises and examples, use the workbook in the back of the book as your template for assessing your persona, promise and building your personal brand statement.

I strongly encourage you to perform your own personal brand assessment survey. Come up with a list of friends and/or colleagues who could answer the below (sample) set of questions:

- What do you think are my greatest strengths?
- What is my unique expertise or value that differentiates me?
- How do I come across to others?
- What are the key adjectives that describe my personality?
- What are the weaknesses that may hold me back?

Although it may be intimidating for some of us to reach out to others for their opinions about ourselves, I encourage you to try. Putting some effort into this portion of your assessment strategy will reap immense rewards into crafting your brand management strategy and will lead to worthwhile insights.

Let me stop here and say that Planning and Assessment can occur at the same time. I organize planning as step one, and assessment as step two, mostly to provide you with a framework from where to begin your work.

But the strategies could be worked on hand in hand. Although let me caution that it may be helpful to know what your planning goals are first. So that when you are conducting your assessment, and you are learning what words people use to describe you, what they think your strengths are, etc, you can better frame that information and compare it to your goals. If you know where you want to go, it will be easier to analyze, frame, and understand how to put into context the information of how others see and perceive you now.

For example, your goal may be to increase your visibility and credibility because you want to become the director of your department. You conduct your assessment, and you learn that most of your colleagues only describe you as organized and a good project manager. Knowing where you want to go, which is to become a director, helps you put into context the information you've just learned, because you now know that you need to change perception, so that they see you with a different skillset to match that of a director and not just a team member. You will need to help them see you as a leader, manager, etc *(we talk about how to promote yourself under strategy three, expression,).* If you aren't sure what your goal is, it may be harder to find meaning in how people see and describe you.

2A. What is a persona? (See Page 47 of the Workbook Section)
A persona describes who you are and the qualities that make you, YOU. They are your distinct attributes, characteristics, vision and values.

A persona includes the following:
- Attributes
- Characteristics
- Vision
- Values

Helpful resources for uncovering your persona:
- Friends, family, and colleagues
- Hobbies, interests, and passions

Helping Questions:
>What are my strongest attributes?
>What am I passionate about?
>What motivates me?

2B. What is a Promise? (See Page 50 of the Workbook Section)

It is your unique value. How does someone benefit from working with you? It is what sets you apart. Do you offer unparalleled quality? Do you provide quick turnarounds? Do you enjoy solving complex problems?

Helpful resources for uncovering your promise:
- Performance reviews
- Project and product feedback
- Team assignments

Helping questions:
>What makes me unique?
>What results do people experience when working with me? What can I help others to achieve?
>How do people introduce me?

Now let's put your hard work into action by creating your personal brand story.

2C. What is a personal brand statement? (See Page 53 of the Workbook Section)

A personal brand statement is a short pitch (1-3 sentences) that communicates your **value** (what you are the best at), your **audience** (who you serve), and your **promise** (how you perform your value uniquely).

Why do you need it and how do you use it?

You need a personal brand statement to help you communicate to the world, clearly, succinctly, and briefly what it is you want them to know about your brand. All companies with a product to sell develop different value proposition statements (or also known as positioning statements or unique selling propositions) that help define what they are selling, to whom, and why it's of value to their target audience. You, as a product for the brand called YOU, are doing the same thing!

How do you use a personal branding statement? You use it for your LinkedIn profile summary, on your resume, your biography, and just about anywhere that needs a succinct and brief explanation of who you are and what you bring to the world.

What a personal brand statement is NOT.
Your personal brand statement is **NOT** your job title, personal mission statement, career objectives or life's purpose. These items may be part of your brand statement but they do not encompass the purpose of a brand statement. *See workbook page 62 for example.*

> *"You're not defined by your job title and you're not confined by your job description." - Tom Peters*

In other words: Link your strongest attribute *(Persona)* and the results it created for someone *(Promise)*
into a story.

3. Last, but not least...***EXPRESSION. OR how will you PROMOTE your brand? (See Page 59 of the Workbook Section)***
Objectives

- How will you tell Your Brand Story?
- Develop Brand Ambassadors
- Do you need a mentor?

Link your strongest attribute **(Persona)** and the results it created for someone **(Promise)** into a story. Tell your story to one of your Brand Ambassadors **(Promotion).**

What are the ways you can tell your brand story? (sample ideas)

- Present at Conferences
- Attend Conferences
- Volunteer at work, in your community
- One-on-one conversations
- Blog
- LinkedIn Articles
- Email signature
- Local Meet-up
- Interest Groups
- Networking events

Three things you can do today!

- Update your LinkedIn Profile –use your personal brand statement for your profile description.
- If you need a mentor, write 1-3 names of people you can call today and ask out for coffee!
- Conduct your personal brand assessment survey *(See Page 60 of the Workbook Section)*

Personal Brand Spotlight:

Michelle Obama, former First Lady of the United States, was able to step out of her husband's shadow, and build her own personal brand. It can be difficult to achieve your own identity, especially when you are married to a powerful brand, while at the same time, maintain support for your husband's very, public, and high-level role as an elected official. But, in my opinion, her personal brand blossomed before our eyes.

Through action and authentic thought, in a very short time, she built her own identity, and a strong personal brand, outside of the shadow of her husband, the President of the United States. I would argue, she built a stronger brand more so than other former, First Ladies. No disrespect to any of our former First Ladies, as they also used their public platform for the greater good. But I would say, Michelle Obama really stretched the boundaries of her role to become her own brand, outside of her role and brand as the First Lady.

Michelle Obama's brand is identified with her many independently started philanthropic initiatives (from health/nutrition programs for kids to global women's issues), visits to communities around the world, relationships with major leaders, and participation in events big, small, political, and some purely for entertainment (remember the time Obama danced with Jimmy Fallon on "The Tonight Show"? Or was seen shopping "undercover" at Target?). She became renowned for her incredible public speaking skills constructing articulate, engaging, empathetic, and relevant conversation. Her brand has come to represent inspiration, courage, and power. Her fashion style even became part of her brand. Although building your personal brand takes time and commitment, and admittedly she had a communications team behind her to help build a strategy, she still had to be willing and interested to find ways of expressing her authentic self and brand purpose through her role. She's an ideal transcendence of a personal brand over a few years.

4 - MANAGING YOUR STRENGTHS AND WEAKNESSES AS PART OF YOUR PERSONAL BRAND

"Don't Be Scared To Present The Real You To The World, Authenticity Is At The Heart Of Success."
– Unknown

There is a great article and video on the Lean In website (https://leanin.org/), by Marcus Buckingham, the world's foremost authority on strengths-based management and leadership in the workforce. Mr. Buckingham has a very helpful explanation of what strengths and weaknesses mean to us, how we have been programmed to define them, and basically how we should re-program ourselves to redefine what they mean.

Why is this important to you?

Because if you are building or managing your brand, and you want to communicate your value proposition to the world, you need to understand what makes YOU unique. How is your uniqueness useful to the world? How will you promote that uniqueness?

During my personal branding workshops I am commonly asked questions around the concept of strengths and weaknesses, such as, "Should I work on improving my weaknesses first, then focus on my strengths?" "Is there a right or wrong way on what I should do next in order to improve my brand—work on my weaknesses or promote my strengths?" "Are weaknesses really a "weakness" versus just some skills I need to improve?"

What I liked about Mr. Buckingham's exercise is that he redefines our traditional definitions of these two concepts. Strength is not necessarily only what you are good at. Weakness is not necessarily a negative characteristic. Instead, he wants us to think about strengths and weaknesses, not as skills, but as actions or activities. Strength is an activity that strengthens you, hence, weakness is an activity that weakens you. He says, "You have some activities or tasks you do well, but hate doing. You have the ability; you can do it. You just wish you never had to do it again because it drains you."

He provides a series of questions, as part of an exercise, of how to be more aware of your strengths so you can better define and thus communicate them.

In this exercise, think about the following-
- What activity makes you feel successful and in control?
- What activities do you look forward to doing?
- Do you feel like you grew or grow from that activity?
- Even if you are tired after doing that activity, do you still feel a sense of accomplishment?

Your answers should fall under one or all of the below categories, which is summarized by his assessment process as "SIGN:"

- **S**uccess: you feel in control when you are doing this activity.
- **I**nstinct: you look forward to doing the activity.
- **G**rowth: you enjoy learning and are focused on this activity.
- **N**eeds: you feel a sense of fulfillment after the activity is over.

For assessing your weaknesses—what activities makes you feel drained and bored? Additionally he offers some tips on how to manage your weaknesses. Such as, pair up with a colleague who enjoys the activity that you do not enjoy. Change your mind set about the activities you don't enjoy, and search for some positive aspects about it. You may not have a choice about whether or not to do them, so how can you infuse your strengths into this activity so that it no longer contributes to weakness? Ensure others know your strengths, so that you are not asked, nor are you offering, to work on activities that contribute to a weakness.
So how should you manage STRENGTHS and WEAKNESSES as part of your brand?

As a personal example of a weakness, I don't like taking meeting minutes.

It's a mundane task and I'm an action, big picture person. But, when I have to volunteer for this type of task, I change my mindset about the task, and use my writing and organization skills and pretend I'm writing marketing copy. The result, is that the meeting participants will receive, short, concise, action-oriented meeting minutes (versus perhaps verbatim meeting minutes).

I know this particular task is a weakness for me because it drains me. But I know I have to do these types of tasks sometimes, for the good of my reputation and organization. So I suck it up, as they say, and start writing. I don't necessarily announce to my colleagues there are tasks, I have the ability to do but simply don't enjoy doing, rather, whenever I get a chance to promote my strengths, I get in there and show my enthusiasm for doing or volunteering to do other more enjoyable tasks.

I want to be known for my preferred strengths, but I don't shy away from performing those activities that I consider my weaknesses, because, for instance, I don't want people to think that I'm not a team player. We must all make choices and consider our brand in the totality of circumstances.

What can you do to let others know about your strengths? What weaknesses do you have that on the one hand, you definitely are unable or incapable of performing? What are those other weaknesses that you don't want to perform, but still should do them, for the good of the team or the cause?

I would encourage you to watch Mr. Buckingham's video [VI] and also use his study guide [VII] to go through the exercise of studying his revised concepts of strengths and weaknesses, and apply these new definitions to help define or redefine your personal brand.

Personal Brand Spotlight:

Stan Lee, writer and **Jack Kirby**, illustrator, two of history's most famous duos for inventing some of the most popular comic book characters, provides us with a cautionary tale. An example of someone who took charge of their brand, and another who let others brand him. It's an example of someone who crafted a strategy to manage their brand, and another who may not have  assessed his persona, and understood his weaknesses, so that he could find ways to express his brand in ways that fit his personality and style best.

AMC's Robert Kirkman's Secret History of Comics [VIII], "The Mighty Misfits who Made Marvel" tells the story of Stan Lee, who effectively became the face of Marvel comics, whereas Jack Kirby, although he was well respected in their professional circles, never received the same attention or credit, at least in the eyes of the public. While Lee was a showman, who was great at interviews, and dealing with the press and the public, Kirby was the opposite, introverted, not good in interviews, so he fell into the shadow of Stan Lee. To this day there is still an open debate, of which partner was more influential to the development of these beloved characters such as Spider-Man, The Fantastic Four, The Avengers, The Incredible Hulk, X-Men, Lee or Kirby? Was it Kirby's innovative drawings, or was it Lee's bravado in writing?

Most of us are not aware of this partnership because Lee had the ability to communicate and tell his stories, promote his brand much stronger than Kirby, and so...most of us may think that Lee was the sole inventor of these great comic characters. One could say that Kirby could have benefitted from a brand assessment, and brand strategy. Maybe it would have been different if Kirby would have been able to plan, assess and learn how to express his brand and his accomplishments. Imagine if Kirby would have used drawing to express his brand? I admit, I only knew of Stan Lee, not because I'm a fan of comic book characters per say, but because he has been a guest star on the hit CBS show "The Big Bang Theory." So when I watched this documentary series, I was both surprised and sad to learn about this personal brand tragedy for one of the members of this dynamic duo. Two brilliant individuals, epic collaboration, but one person took charge of his brand, and the other person could not figure out how to brand himself. The latter person, Kirby, faded into the obscurity of popular culture.

5 - MANAGE YOUR BRAND, 15 MINUTES A DAY!

"If You're Not Branding Yourself, You Can Be Sure Others Do It For You."
— Unknown

DAILY TASKS TO MANAGE YOUR BRAND

I believe that in order to manage your brand you need to build brand management into your everyday consciousness. Below is a suggested daily task list that you could think about and implement on a daily (or weekly basis)--—but you should consider taking 15 mins each day to reflect on how you are managing your brand.

Take these activities as suggestions, and ideas, and match it to your style and needs. Allow this list of recommended activities to help you begin the process of incorporating, intentional, daily actions to keep your personal brand management top of mind.

> MONDAY: Is there anything in your persona, promise and promotion strategy that you haven't worked on lately? Does your personal branding statement need a quick review/update?
>
> TUESDAY: Visit your LinkedIn profile. Do you need a makeover or to conduct maintenance? Here's a few tasks to consider doing on a weekly basis:
> - Is your headshot up to date—do you need a professional headshot? Upload a background image(s).
> - Change your headline to keywords that represent your professional strengths. (This is not a place for your job title).

- Have you updated your profile to reflect any professional or personal milestones?
- Is your work history and volunteer activity up to date?
- Have you asked for recommendations or given recommendations?

WEDNESDAY: Make your brand consistent (across all platforms online and offline). For example, if your name is Jose, but are known as Joe, and your online profiles use both names, then your brand is not consistent. Is your professional headshot the same across all platforms? Are you keywords or keyword themes the same across your social media platforms?

THURSDAY: Align with other strong brands. Did you join any groups this week? Were you strategic in whom you invited to connect with this week? Check your groups for possible discussions of interest and comment where appropriate. Have you shared any articles on LinkedIn that support your brand? Did you make any pitches at work to promote your work?

FRIDAY: Build your network. Create a list of people to reach out to; bring your offline relationships online. Start with your colleagues, community/volunteer network, classmates, etc. Look at your calendar--who did you meet this week that you can send a LinkedIn invitation?

SATURDAY: Have you volunteered to do something that supports your brand purpose?

SUNDAY: Review, Renew and Develop Yourself. Remember your brand management needs to be constant, but it also won't happen overnight. So what can you do this coming week?

Managing your brand is a purposeful journey...it takes time, patience, and lots of self-love. Commit yourself to set aside 15 minutes a day to grow and manage your brand. Additionally, keep your personal brand front and center as you set your intentions for meetings you participate in, your interactions with others, and decisions you make.

Side Note: As long as we are talking about weaving your personal branding intentions into your daily actions, I would encourage you to also think about how you can weave in the power of positive thinking and setting goals for yourself on an annual basis. A recent favorite book, "#POSITIVITY" IX, by Phil Hellmuth Jr., 14 time world champion poker player, provides actionable tips for how to incorporate positivity into everything you do. That includes writing out your life and yearly goals for yourself, and taping them to your bathroom mirror so that you see them, and read them every day. He shares that as a child, his mother taped a sign to their bathroom mirror that read:

"You are what you think;
You become what you think;
What you think becomes reality."

He credits this early influence of positive thinking and goal setting with helping him achieve his success as a world-class poker player and bestselling author.

When I read the chapter called "Bathroom Mirror, Your Yearly Goals," I took this action to heart, and below is a picture of my goals that I have up on my bathroom mirror. You'll see that my number one goal is to write a personal branding book. (The second sheet on the wall are my daily affirmations...to help focus my positive thinking. Mr. Hellmuth also gives you tips on how to incorporate affirmations into your daily life).

So—if your goal is to improve your personal brand management, then write it down on your goals list and put it up in your bathroom!

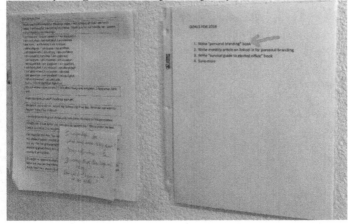

Personal Brand Spotlight:

Maya Angelou is an example of an evolving, but enduring brand experience. She self-described her brand as a "A Global Renaissance Woman." Dr. Angelou was an actress, singer, dancer, poet, memoirist, novelist, educator, dramatist, producer, historian, filmmaker and civil rights activist. Despite her various professional roles, her brand promise, the essence of who she was remained constant. The article by Tamara Jacobs, "Maya Angelou, The Power of an Evolving Brand," describes, that at her core, Dr. Angelou's "brand and body of work stood for words and actions that stir souls, energize bodies, liberate minds and heal hearts." [x]

One of her famous quotes, "I've learned that people will forget what you said, people will forget what you did, but people will never forget how you made them feel," embodies the idea that a brand is an experience. Forget about taglines, logos, and product colors…how do you want people to feel during and after an interaction with you? What is your brand experience?

Additionally her experience with gender and racial discrimination became part of her brand story, which in turn, allowed her body of work to exude empathy, compassion and understanding for others. Her story validated and gave others permission to own and share their story. Some of you may have an untold story, but when you get clarity around your brand, as Dr. Angelou did, your story tells itself.

6 - FINDING A PURPOSE FOR YOUR PERSONAL BRAND

"If You Can't Find Your Own Center And Love For Yourself,
Nothing Else Works."
– Chris Brogan

I was blessed to have received an award from the Latina Coalition of Silicon Valley, called the "Sisterhood Award," which is awarded to an individual who exemplifies and represents the organization's mission to provide leadership and mentorship in their community through civic engagement.

Receiving this award was a great honor, and it reminded me how important it is for all of us to find a purpose for our personal brand. In my comments to the audience, I said that I believed this award came with great responsibility. I believe we have a purpose in this life. Besides finding and fulfilling our own dreams and finding joy in our lives, I believe we have a responsibility to help each other.

My husband and I share a personal philosophy of helping improve the lives of others. He may have learned that from his father, his role model. For me, I think it has always come innately, and it probably became more defined when I attended Santa Clara University—where the Jesuit philosophy of "men and women in services for others" really spoke to me—so it's become a deep part of me. Personal branding is a self-centered process and there is nothing wrong with that. That self-focused process has to occur first in order to figure out who we are and how to communicate it to the world. But it's also about building purpose to your brand that stands for more just than yourself. It's about figuring out ways that you can give back to your community.

Giving back to those in need -- in your community, around the world, to the next generation or whatever fits your brand. Just as I said in the introduction to this book, you don't have to be a CEO or serve in elected office to have a brand, and you certainly don't have to be in any one of these types of positions in order to give back. It could be as simple as becoming a mentor, a volunteer, give out referrals, join a volunteer group through work, etc. My personal purpose is about building the capacity of others, and contributing to their development…it's about seeing potential and helping others reach theirs. So I use my professional skills to help others communicate their value, courage and find their voice.

Think about your passion(s) and that should be the foundation for your giving. It is not *how much* you give, but *how much love* you put into giving. It's only natural that you will care about this, and not so much about that, and that's OK. It should not be simply a matter of choosing the right thing, but also a matter of choosing what is right for you.

So as the old Chinese proverb says—"If you want happiness for a lifetime, help somebody."

Your action item—think about how you can add purpose to your personal brand. How can you find a purpose to your brand so that you stand for something more than just yourself? Create a way to give back. Find a way to make  your mark, and make it a part of your plans. How can you achieve personal success, but also find ways to lift up those around you?

Key messaging, having a **personal branding statement** [XIII] and being able to **articulate your purpose** is all part of embodying and living your personal brand.

> *"Giving back is as good for you as it is for those you are helping, because giving gives you purpose. When you have a purpose-driven life, you're a happier person"* — *Goldie Hawn*

Personal Brand Spotlight:

Sometimes our brand purpose can stem from tragedies or challenges in our lives. Sometimes we find our passions come from untold stories in our lives. Sometimes it will take years for these untold stories to become part of our consciousness, and be able to speak about them aloud. **Elizabeth Smart**, nationally known for her 9-month abduction at the age of 14, is to me, an example of someone who found her brand purpose from a tragic experience. Understandably so, it took her years for her to find her voice and thus be able to tell her story. I heard Elizabeth Smart speak at an annual YWCA Silicon Valley fundraising luncheon, and I was mesmerized by her presence, calm, poise and the inner light that she radiated. I thought—what an extraordinary human being, who after 15 years since her abduction, she's made it her mission to speak publicly about her ordeal and advocate for victims of kidnapping and sexual assaults. As part of expressing her brand, she's published and produced her autobiographical book and film. Elizabeth Smart, for me, is someone who learned how to own her story, make it a part of her brand, so that when her name is mentioned, I no longer think of just her tragedy, I now also think of her strength.

7 - SELF-PROMOTION IS EASIER *WHEN*...

"Your Brand Is What People Say About You When You Are Not In The Room."
— Jeff Bezos

Self-promotion is easier *when* you understand the difference between self-promotion versus bragging. Is it relevant to the conversation at hand and/or does it make someone feel less?

Let me insert an important "cultural and gender difference" note here--I understand, that for some cultures, for example, in my Latino culture, some of us are brought up to be humble, and to promote yourself in any way will be considered a braggart. There are also gender differences, in terms of how women and men promote themselves. For some women, (and I can attest to this) it tends to be much easier to share about our interests and passions, but much harder to share about our professional accomplishments. On the other hand, it's easier for men, to speak about their professional accomplishments, versus their interests and passions. So there are some cultures or gender differences that may not have allowed us, up to now, to feel either okay or comfortable to self-promote. So for those of you that fall into either of those categories, we will need to do some extra work to get over that "cultural or gender wall," and learn how to promote yourself without shame or embarrassment. The key is understanding your paradigm and learning what to do about it.

Thus...hopefully self-promotion will be easier when...*you read the rest of this chapter!*

I have had to learn (and it's constant practice) how to promote my brand. I may be an extrovert, who likes to talk to people, gets energy from other people, and can talk to anyone about almost anything, but it was always hard to talk about myself.   I have had to learn how to promote my personal brand inside my place of work and within my networks outside of work and even in my own family. When I teach my personal branding workshops, inevitably, this question always comes up—"how do I promote myself or brand without sounding like I'm bragging?" The answer is—you have to turn self-promotion into communication where you share information as a form of giving back. Yes, that means it can't be some random comment about how great you are at something, that doesn't relate to the conversation at hand.

So first, self-promotion is easier when you consider it to be information-sharing in a way that helps people see how you might be able to help them. When you are getting ready to share something about yourself and feel that you can't-- tell yourself that you are  merely educating, sharing information about your skills, accomplishments, and at end of the conversation, make sure you end it by commenting that you would be happy to help them.

You want your communication to be as much about you, as the person you are you speaking to…this is about relationship building, and (good) relationships need to be reciprocal in their benefit. Also, remember, this person could be your next brand ambassador (a brand ambassador is someone who speaks highly of you, your strengths, your value when you are not in the room) so what kind of impression do you want to leave with them? On the other hand, I define bragging as sharing about yourself, your achievements, etc., in a way that makes others feel less than you. Ask yourself, why do you want to share this information with the other person?

Now, sometimes, I understand, you want to share good news, success on projects, with friends and colleagues. That's great, and you should, and if they are caring friends and colleagues, they should also celebrate you. But when you are sharing things about yourself, because you know, it's merely to self-promote yourself to be liked, to show-off, to make a person feel inferior to you…that's bragging. We all know instinctively when we are doing this…because we've done it, and your ego may get a little larger at

that moment, but after the fact, you probably lost a brand ambassador.
As an example, I can say "I'm the best marketing expert on personal brands in the Bay Area." Is that bragging? It definitely feels inauthentic to say, so it won't work because I have a hard time saying it powerfully. But, alternatively, I can say "I'm passionate about helping leaders create and market their personal brands. My clients see huge impact when they learn how to create and action their brand." This feels more like I'm sharing, and it feels right to even offer to help the person I'm speaking to. So in sharing--the first sentence is about you, the second sentence is about how you serve others. When we share ourselves and believe in our message, it's more credible and service-oriented to the audience.

Good networking, good communication, good relationships, have to be reciprocal in benefit. There has to be a "win-win" result for both parties. Promote yourself by finding similarities versus differences in others. Start conversations with the desire to learn more about the other person's journey. How can you communicate your accomplishments, skills, and experience to help and benefit other people?

8 - HOW TO SELF-PROMOTE WITHOUT GUILT …

"Too Many People Overvalue What They Are Not and
Undervalue What They Are."
— Malcolm Forbes

So, self-promotion is easier when you consider it to be information-sharing in a way that helps people see how you might be able to help them. The most appropriate question to ask **yourself when you** share **your accomplishments** is "what is my intention here"? If you are already grounded in who you are "self-promotion" is about sharing yourself, sharing the work you passionately care about, sharing the contributions of others, and serving the organization. Doesn't feel so uncomfortable does it?

Don't forget—in order to accomplish the art of self-promotion, first you need to help others understand your persona, promise and brand statement *(See Page 59 of the Workbook Section)* Remember you need to be intentional in how you communicate your skills and the value you bring, rather than hoping others will figure it out on their own.

Self-promotion is an art and a science. It's an art because you have to move around this task intuitively, know when to change strategies, but it needs to come from a genuine place inside of you. But self-promotion is also a science because you have to build a plan. You need to practice it, be consistent in your messaging, strategic, and purposeful.
Additionally, as I mentioned in the last chapter, I know, from personal experience, that many women may feel uncomfortable talking about their accomplishments and promoting themselves directly. But there are ways to show your areas of expertise when promoting your brand and not feel guilty or second guess whether you are bragging or just promoting your

accomplishments in an authentic manner. Let's learn about some tactical ideas you can use to promote your brand without guilt.

Find a mentor. Do you need some help from seasoned professionals who can help guide your continued growth in your field or career? All you need is someone who's willing to share their knowledge, provide guidance, and be available to answer questions once in a while. Treat them to a cup of coffee and thank them. So who could you call today that can serve as your mentor?

Start to develop brand ambassadors. These are the folks who, when you are not in the room, will be able to speak about your strengths, experience, and generally your value, and in turn help promote your brand. How do you develop brand ambassadors? Remember our last chapter…self-promotion versus bragging… well…make sure you are cognizant of how you self-promote, and make sure you are building reciprocity in those interactions and communications. How can you help them? Remember every opportunity you have to interact with someone is an opportunity to leave a lasting impression, which could be negative or positive. So treat every interaction as if it's the first or last impression you want to leave with someone about yourself.

Become your own industry expert. You should also seek to be visible outside of your workplace. Are you really passionate about a subject area? Think about starting a blog, writing articles for LinkedIn, volunteering to present at conferences, etc. With the exception of writing a blog, I have done all of those other activities in the past few years. For example, when I hear of a non-profit doing professional development workshops for their members, I volunteer to do a free personal branding workshop for them. From there, people have liked my workshops, and the word has spread, more invitations to teach my workshops have come in, which eventually has led me to this write this book and my workbook.

Keep your brand consistent offline and online.

What's your image on social media? Be strategic and consistent on LinkedIn, Twitter, Facebook, or whichever social platform you use. Use those platforms to communicate about what you want to be known for …which should be about your

"According to your LinkedIn profile you're a focused, disciplined achiever. According to your Facebook photos you love Jack Daniels and are pretty comfortable with your body."

persona, promise and brand statement, or brand purpose, versus your wild parties with your friends on weekends.

Take advantage of your performance reviews. Talk about your results with your manager; take advantage of your performance reviews to show the good work you've accomplished throughout the year. Send a weekly or monthly email to your manager with accomplishments for that month. Remember, when you are successful, your manager is also successful. The only way your manager will know about the good things you are doing, is to let them know about them.

Additionally, is there a newsletter at work where you can submit ideas for content related to the work (and your brand) you are doing for the company? What projects are you working on that benefit the entire organization that you can share an update, discuss the timeline, or make yourself available for questions, etc? Can you volunteer for any projects?

Other ideas:

- Volunteer: remember **Chapter 6** about finding a purpose for your brand? You can help others while simultaneously helping to promote your brand. But remember, volunteer work should be genuine and it should come from a place of care and passion…otherwise, people will see right through you.
- One-on-one conversation: get to know people, ask them about their personal and professional journeys, build rapport within your network, and in turn, you'll have the opportunity to chat about your journey and your brand.
- LinkedIn profile: use this tool as your personal website. Do you have a professional headshot? Have you maximized the profile to include as much as possible about your personal and professional experience?
- Email signature: Make sure your email signature includes your title and contact information. If you use an email for personal communications, make sure that also has your phone, your LinkedIn profile page link, etc. Don't forget—you also need to email impeccably—that can be your first impression with a potential brand ambassador.
- Local Meet-up Interest Groups: start your own meet-up group, or build your own network of like-minded professionals who can help each other grow and provide support. It doesn't have to be anything formal. Start by building a small network that meets once

in a while casually. My husband has a friend who started one such network. He calls them his "band of brothers," and it's a group of men, from all backgrounds, who are high-level executives, and they get together quarterly for dinner. They talk about the news and issues of the day, as well as, have started to help each other in their respective fields with contacts and support.

- Networking events: What (strategic) organizations can you join that provide opportunities to network with its members? What organizations can you join that match up with your career goals, growth, and/or personal passions?

There is so much more in the way of self-promotion opportunities that can be genuine for you and educational for others...this chapter is just a starting point—whatever you choose to do, remember to be creative, be authentic, and be helpful to others.

9 - REINVENTING YOUR BRAND—YES IT CAN BE DONE!

"Life Isn't About Finding Yourself. Life Is About Creating Yourself."
—George Bernhard Shaw

All brands change over time. In fact, as you grow, your brand grows. It's a continual process. I always ask in my personal branding workshops-- "What happens to your brand when you retire?" It changes. "What happens to your brand when you die?" It changes, but you still have a brand. People will remember you for a few key things that were part of your legacy in their lives. With some luck, and hopefully you did your job of branding yourself consistently, those things they remember you by, will be things you would want them to remember!

As I mentioned in the introduction to this book, I shared why personal branding is such a personal topic for me. I too, had to experience rebranding for myself. Building your brand or reinventing your brand takes risk, courage, and focus. After a very public image crisis experience, which left my brand damaged——and frankly with perceptions of my brand that just were simply not true——I had to reinvent my brand. I was ready for the challenge and work related to reinventing my brand. But first I had to develop my pathway to branding. What was my goal? What did I want to be known for? How did I want people to describe me?

For me, it became crystal clear at some point in my branding assessment work that I wanted to be known as a successful marketing professional and community volunteer, mentor and advocate. To accomplish that, I built an intentional and purposeful plan, that included along that journey, getting my Masters Degree in Integrated Marketing Communications, becoming an adjunct faculty member teaching marketing in higher education, and finding time to volunteer for organizations that I believe in, and am passionate about their mission. As I and my brand evolved, so has my plan and strategy evolved. Different goals may take longer than others to be achieved, so I again invite you to be patient, but don't be afraid to try, fail, and keep going.

We can all change our brand...

There are many examples in this world of people and organizations that were able to reinvent their brand. Remember Martha Stewart? In 2004, she was convicted on charges of conspiracy [XI] and making false statements to investigators pertaining to insider trading. She served five months in prison. Do you think her brand was damaged? Is her brand still strong? Although her brand may have been damaged, for a short time, her brand recovered and is now stronger than ever. A few years ago, Martha Stewart Living Omnimedia merged with Sequential Brands Group. Stewart is currently the chief creative officer of Sequential Brands and a member of its board. Why is her brand stronger than it ever was? Perhaps for three reasons—she had a clear sense of her persona, promise and strategy for promotion. She's quoted in a 2016 article by CNBC as saying, "A person in trouble that doesn't believe she or he is guilty, is a strong person, and I learned how to make lemonade out of lemons," Stewart said. "I'm looking towards the future. I'm an optimist still, and I only see good for the Martha Stewart brand." Of course, I understand that she had a team to help her get her brand back on track, but her perseverance, clear sense of her brand goal, value, are good reasons why her brand is still strong. Including, as important is her product brand promise of excellence, high-quality, trusted content which is still of interest and an inspiration to her consumers.

How can you rebrand yourself?

Focus on those activities and strengths that put you in the best light of your target audience. Figure out what it is you want to be known for? Are you a stay-at-home mom or dad who now wants to jump back into their career? Do you want to change careers? Think about your audience, what will they be looking for in your resume? How do you communicate your experience and value you bring? I have a friend who was a stay-at-home mom for seven years. When she was looking to get back into the workforce, she was branding herself as "a stay-at-home mom, (highlighting past skills from past jobs), coming back into the workforce." But that wasn't getting any interest from prospective employers, so instead she realized she needed to promote her brand for what she wanted to be, and match that to her volunteer, and (part-time) contract work in community and public relations (that she had done while being a stay-at-home mom). She needed to update her perception of herself, her strengths and skills, and start to articulate what was most important to her prospective employers. But let me also say, that stay at home mom and dads, are also a brand, and you should own that title proudly. But as this book emphasizes, depending on your goal and target audience, you will need to cater your message and story to attract the interest and action of your audience.

Focus on where you want to go, not where you have been. This goes back to my emphasis of understanding, first and foremost, your branding goal. Know what you want. Know where to get it. These could include but are not limited to: Visibility; Preference; Credibility; Engagement; Influence; Perception, etc. Who is your audience and who do you want to influence? What do they care about? Or how could you help them solve a need? Back to my friend, the stay-at-home mom, now a successful community relations professional, she had to focus on her most relevant part time work/volunteer experience, own it, articulate it, and not emphasize her last seven years as "Mom CEO."

Expand your network to broaden you brand. With your brand changing, your network may also need to change. Remember we are multidimensional in our activities and pursuits, so we may need more than one network to recognize our brand. Your current network may not be the right one anymore to acknowledge your new brand as a public relations executive. Remember, you are not a stay-at-home mom anymore. You don't have to drop the old networks, but if you're serious about re-branding yourself in a specific way, broaden your network to new people who never knew the old you and don't have to be convinced. As your brand evolves, so does your network, and you will need to be conscientious and purposeful in knowing when you need to expand those circles.

This next section of the chapter still continues with the theme of reinventing your brand, but with a twist. Find a passion (project) that can serve as an extension of your brand. Passion projects are just as important for your professional growth, and that also becomes part of your brand story. Remember my "stay-at-home" mom friend, what if when she was trying to promote herself, she had told her prospective employers that she had led a successful, (passion) volunteer project/effort at her children's school that improved the nutritional food options for the students. That passion project required leadership, project management and communication skills. Her brand is no longer of a stay-at-home, it's one of leader, change-agent, and community advocate. *What are you passionate about that can be an extension of your brand and that can help you communicate your value and brand story?*

For me, my passion project involves dogs…specifically, changing the pejorative view of the way people view pit bulls.

So…let's talk about dog brands…

Yes, even dogs have brands. After all, aren't they "man's best friend?" What do you think of pit bulls? Dangerous animals or nanny dogs?

Once upon a time, pit bulls were America's preferred family dog. Dubbed the "nanny dog," they were trusted to safeguard the family's young children. They had positive images. In the first half of the 20th century, one of the most recognized dogs was a pit bull named Petey. The dog who starred in a long series of "Little Rascals" films opposite children. Other famous pit bulls, include Sgt. Stubby, a WWI hero dog.

So how did their brands change for the negative? The change only occurred fairly recently. The negative image can be traced to a 1987 [XII] Sports Illustrated cover photo and story. The story's sensationalism caused a surge in interest in the dog from unsavory characters such as drug dealers and people who organized dog fights for sport. Pit Bulls, however, are not the first, nor only, breed to ever suffer from a negative brand problem. At various times, German shepherds and Rottweilers also suffered from negative images. The consequences of this negative brand image are serious since they include blanket bans and even an increased rate of abandonment and euthanasia at shelters.

Just this history alone should be strong evidence that it's not the breed that's the problem; it's how they're treated by the humans who are responsible for them. Many organizations and tv stars, such as Cesar

Millan, from the TV show, *The Dog Whisperer*, have contributed to the new popularity of national pit bull awareness, and its related national campaigns. But that's not enough...and it's never enough, because **people forget if you don't keep reminding them of your value, strengths, and overall brand.** To counter the years of negative perception in society, and because people forget (we have a very, short attention span nowadays—8 seconds— true and based on research!), these national awareness campaigns will need to continue for a long time. Similarly, your personal branding efforts will need to continue to infinity because you have to keep reminding your networks of those things you want to be known for, and how you want them to describe you.

So, meet my passion branding project...Murphy "Pittie With A Purpose"...helping to change the brand perception of pit bulls...helping to change minds one person at a time. His purpose is to show you that with training and love "pitties" are friendly and loving dogs. Murphy is a goodwill ambassador to the pit bull brand!

Murphy—our "pittie with a purpose."

36

Murphy owns his personal brand—and he wants you to know him as loving, and friendly-- ...that's how he's reinventing and promoting his personal brand.

How can you reinvent or redefine your personal brand? What do you want your new brand to say about you?

What are you passionate about that can be an extension of your brand and help you communicate your value and brand story?

You can follow Murphy's personal branding adventures on Instagram @murphypittiewithpurpose

10 - SUMMARY

"Branding Demands Commitment; Commitment To Continual Re-Invention; Striking Chords With People To Stir Their Emotions; And Commitment To Imagination. It Is Easy To Be Cynical About Such Things, Much Harder To Be Successful."
— Sir Richard Branson

Personal branding as a term was first used in 1997 in Tom Peters' Fast Company article, in which he said: "We are CEOs of our own companies: Me Inc. To be in business today, our most important job is to be head marketer for the brand called You."

You've learned in this book, and with our proceeding workbook, that we need to be active participants, purposeful in our actions, to communicate to the world, our brand, our promise and purpose.

Developing your personal brand requires you to find your authentic voice. The process of creating one develops who you are -- the unique you – "BRAND YOU." When you find your voice, and your audiences start to react positively, that builds your self-confidence and self-esteem and allows you to find yourself in a meaningful way.

Whether you are trying to build your business, find a job, get noticed by the press, impress vendors, attract influential contacts or simply make new successful friends, a powerful, attractive and visible brand is the key. And it's also key to building your reputation, credibility and most importantly, being successful in your professional and personal life.
There are thousands of resources that can help you figure out how to best own and manage your personal brand. My goal was to outline a simple method that could speak to you, that is easy to understand and thus implement. I will consider this book a success, even if only one of the methods or strategies spoke to you! I hope you feel that with this book and

workbook, that your personal branding work is manageable, and that it's something you can start now and also, help others to think about and practice. This book is a start, a foundation for you to build upon, and you need to learn, apply it, adjust and keep going.

After reading this book and completing the workbook exercises, I want you to truly feel that you can take charge of your brand. I want you to feel that you truly own your brand, that you have the tools to manage it, and the confidence to promote it!

The confidence to promote it...yes you have the confidence! We need to be less shy about communicating our brand and more strategic and authentic in finding ways to help our brand help others. We all want to be successful, whether it's in our careers, or outside of the office. But the truth is,

"OK, yes, you're a cow. But you're also a dairy consultant, an expert on calcium, and a hay connoisseur to boot!"

in most companies, or organizations, you're probably not going to get ahead just by doing a great job. You need to also build a supportive network and learn how to promote your brand inside and outside of your professional world. But, to get promoted, you first have to promote yourself.

You have to learn how to share your accomplishments, value, and purpose. For most of us, communicating your accomplishments, value and purpose is usually not easy. Personal branding work is not easy. This work and process challenges you to analyze yourself deeply, learn how to communicate and talk about yourself, and be willing to try, fail, and start again. But in order to own and grow your brand, one must do the work...and the workbook provides you a pathway to assess and be able to find the confidence to better understand and communicate your value and purpose. I know it's hard to think about what makes you unique, your values, and attributes, let alone talk about it! But, you must do this work in order to build the confidence necessary to be able to promote yourself and thus your personal brand.

I invite you to continue this personal branding journey—schedule 15-20 minutes a day and work on one of the three branding strategies laid out in this book.

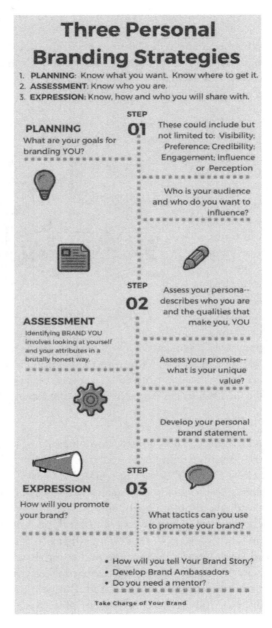

I know you have a great brand to share with the world...now you just need to take charge and let the world know about it! Be confident, be authentic, and be purposeful!

Remember---personal branding is something you manage, not something that just happens.

Your brand is working 24 hours a day; make sure it is communicating what you want. **What have you done for your brand today?**

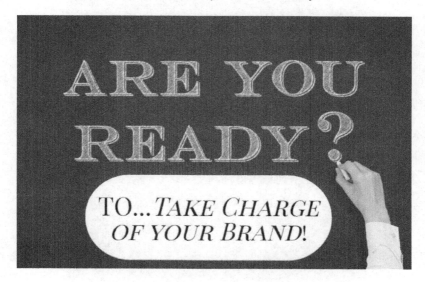

8

PERSONAL BRANDING
YOUR CHECKLIST

1 **PLAN--WHAT'S YOUR GOAL?**
What's your personal branding goal and who is your target audience?

2 **PERSONAL BRAND ASSESSMENT SURVEY**
Conduct your personal brand assessment survey to help you assess/develop your persona, promise and personal brand statement.

3 **ASSESS YOUR PERSONA**
What are those values, attributes, and qualities that make you, YOU?

4 **ASSESS YOUR PROMISE**
What is your unique value?

5 **BUILD YOUR PERSONAL BRAND STATEMENT**
...to help you communicate briefly what it is you want others to know about your brand.

6 **EXPRESSION-HOW WILL YOU PROMOTE YOUR BRAND?**
How will you promote your brand?

7 **PERSONAL BRAND PURPOSE**
How can you find a purpose to your brand so that you stand for something more than just yourself?

8 **TIME ALLOCATION**
Are you willing to allocate 15-20 minutes per day to manage your personal brand?

TAKE CHARGE OF YOUR BRAND

<u>END NOTES</u>

I. Tom Peters, The Brand Called You," Fast Company, http://www.fastcompany.com/28905/brand-called-you

II. https://www.usatoday.com/story/life/books/2013/10/02/author-tom-clancy-dies-at-66/2907629/

III. Lewis Packwood, "The bizarre tale of how Tom Clancy sold his name to videogames," PC Games News, https://www.pcgamesn.com/rainbow-six-siege/tom-clancy-videogames

IV. Laura Vanderkam, " What does Authenticity Really Mean?, " Fast Company, https://www.fastcompany.com/3053566/what-does-authenticity-really-mean

V. Laura Ries, "Build a Brand, Not Just a Career," Forbes, https://www.forbes.com/sites/lisaquast/2012/11/19/build-a-personal-brand-not-just-a-career/#59f1c65a4e69

VI. Video: https://leanin.org/education/know-your-strengths-own-your-strengths-no-one-else-will/?utm_source=Lean+In+Community&utm_campaign=705aea9c60-Circles_May2018&utm_medium=email&utm_term=0_75753fa920-705aea9c60-60536641&mc_cid=705aea9c60&mc_eid=b26912be1d

VII. Marcus Buckingham, "Claiming your Strengths," Discussion Guide https://cdn-media.leanin.org/wp-content/uploads/2013/11/Claiming_Your_Strengths.pdf

VIII. Robert Kirkman's Secret History of Comics, "The Mighty Misfits who made Marvel," Season 1, Episode 1, 2017, https://www.amc.com/shows/robert-kirkmans-secret-history-of-comics

IX. Phil Hellmuth Jr., "#POSITIVITY," 2018

X. Tamara Jacobs, "Maya Angelou: The Power of an Evolving Brand," Huffington Post, https://www.huffingtonpost.com/tamara-jacobs/maya-angelou-the-power-of-an-evolving-brand_b_5447993.html

XI. For clarification--- the crime of "conspiracy" does not exist. conspiracy must be accompanied by an underlying crime. e.g., "conspiracy to commit fraud", etc. Ms. Stewart was found guilty of four counts of obstruction of justice and lying to investigators. https://danielsethics.mgt.unm.edu/pdf/martha%20stewart%20case.pdf

XII. E.M Swift, "The Pitbull Friend And Killer," Sports Illustrated, Vault, July 27, 1987, https://www.si.com/vault/1987/07/27/115813/the-pit-bull-friend-and-killer-is-the-pit-bull-a-fine-animal-as-its-admirers-claim-or-is-it-a-vicious-dog-unfit-for-society)

XIII. Delightful Communications Blog, https://www.delightfulcommunications.com/blog/write-personal-branding-statement/

ADDITIONAL REFERENCE DATA

Alyson Shontell, "Steve Jobs interviewed 20 people to be CEO of Apple and disliked them all — here's the unconventional way John Sculley wowed him and snagged the offer," Business Insider, http://www.businessinsider.com/john-sculley-interview-steve-jobs-apple-ceo-podcast-success-how-i-did-it2017-8

Accompany Blog, "Importance of personal branding," https://www.accompany.com/importance-personal-branding/

Abraham Riesman, "It's Stan Lee's Universe," Vulture, http://www.vulture.com/2016/02/stan-lees-universe-c-v-r.html

Kylie Butler, Inspired Careers Blog, https://inspiredcareerscoaching.com.au/blog/

James Altucher, "Elizabeth Smart: How She Endured Tragedy, Survived and Created Her New Normal," Huffington Post, https://www.huffingtonpost.com/entry/elizabeth-smart-how-she-endured-tragedy-survived_us_5a1088cbe4b023121e0e9350

Sonia Sairaya, "TV Review: Lifetime's 'I Am Elizabeth Smart'," Variety, https://variety.com/2017/tv/reviews/i-am-elizabeth-smart-review-lifetime-1202617906/

Paulette Cohn, "Elizabeth Smart Shares the Truth Behind Her Abduction in Lifetime's I Am Elizabeth Smart," Parade, July 12, 2018 https://parade.com/620120/paulettecohn/elizabeth-smart-shares-the-truth-behind-her-abduction-in-lifetimes-i-am-elizabeth-smart/

<u>HOW TO USE THIS WORKBOOK</u>

This workbook is designed to help you apply the information and knowledge gained from the previous sections and chapters to strengthen your personal brand development. It is a workbook, so do the work and watch your brand strategy really take shape.

EXERCISE 1 – WHAT'S YOUR PERSONA

Objectives:

The purpose of this exercise is to help you
- o Start creating your personal brand
- o Get a sense of the process and approach to develop your personal brand
- o Be clear about who you are and understand how having a strong personal brand can provide professional opportunities

What is a persona?

A persona describes who you are and the qualities that make you, you. They are your distinct attributes, characteristics, vision and values.

A persona includes the following:
- o Attributes
- o Characteristics
- o Vision
- o Values

Helpful resources for uncovering your persona:
- o Friends, family, and colleagues
- o Hobbies, interests, and passions

Helping Questions

1. What are your strongest attributes? List three to five.

| |
| |
| |
| |
| |
| |
| |
| |
| |
| |
| |

2.   What am I passionate about?

3.   What motivates me?

Additional Questions to Consider:

4.   What are my personal values?

5.   Where do I see myself in 5 years?

6.   What is important to me?

7. How would I like to see the world?

8. What contribution would I like to make?

Persona

Helpful Adjectives:

➤ Open mind	➤ Driven	➤ Leadership
➤ Friendly	➤ Passionate	➤ Vision
➤ Determination	➤ Collaborative	➤ Quality
➤ Visionary	➤ Personable	➤ Diversity
➤ Positive	➤ Energetic	➤ Service
➤ Strategic	➤ Friendly	➤ Helping others
➤ Creative	➤ Trust	➤ Education
➤ Present	➤ Courage	➤ Competence
➤ Focused	➤ Respect	➤ Respect
➤ Flexible	➤ Integrity	➤ Responsibility
➤ Inspirational	➤ Passion	➤ Expert
➤ Sense of humor	➤ Innovation	➤ Unflappable
➤ Compassionate	➤ Transparency	➤ Competent
➤ Patient	➤ Adaptability	➤ Giving back
➤ Results-oriented	➤ Reliability	➤ Honesty
➤ Analytical	➤ Accountability	➤ Confident

EXERCISE 2 – WHAT'S YOUR PROMISE

Objectives:

The purpose of this exercise is to help you

- o Develop your unique personal promise of value
- o Understand what other people think they gain by working with you
- o Be clear about why you are the best at what you do

What is a Promise?

It is your unique value. How does someone benefit from working with you? It is what sets you apart. Do you offer unparalleled quality? Do you provide quick turnarounds? Do you enjoy solving complex problems?

Helpful resources for uncovering your promise:

- o Performance reviews
- o Project and product feedback
- o Team assignments

Helping questions

1. What makes me unique?

2. What results do people experience when working with me? What can I help others to achieve?

---

3. What personality characteristics make people interested in me?

Additional Questions to Consider:
4. What makes me stay in my career?

---

5. What types of activities cause me to lose track of time?

---

6. What do I do differently than others in my profession?

---

7. What do I want to help others with?

---

8. Why do people come to me for help?

| |
| |
| |
| |

9. How do people introduce me?

| |
| |
| |
| |

Promise

Consider using Power Phrases:

- "I can..."
- "Because I am good at..."
- "I've had great success with..."
- "I've had great experience..."

- "I was honored..."
- "The funniest thing..."
- "It was so exciting to..."
- "I am best at..."

Examples of things you may have to offer:

- Project Management
- People Management
- Financial or Operation Management
- Technical Expertise
- Strategic Planning
- Managing Conflict
- Creative Problem Solving
- Delivering Presentations
- Decision Making

- Mentoring
- Communication
- Strategic Vision
- Collaboration and Teamwork
- Building and Leading Teams
- Leading Innovation
- Streamlining Processes
- Striving for Results
- Change Management

Fun Adjectives:

- Sophisticated
- Elegant
- Edgy
- Classic
- Business Casual
- Urban
- Artistic
- Innovative

- Technology Savvy
- Worldly
- Cultured
- Colorful
- Conservative
- Academic
- Professional
- Entrepreneurial

EXERCISE 3: CREATE YOUR BRAND STATEMENT

Now let's put your hard work into action by creating your personal brand story.

What is a personal brand statement?

A personal brand statement is a short pitch (1-3 sentences) that communicates your **value** (what you are the best at), your **audience** (who you serve), and your **promise** (how you perform your value uniquely).

What a personal brand statement is NOT.

Your personal brand statement is **NOT** your job title, personal mission statement, career objectives or life's purpose. These items may be part of your brand statement but they do not encompass the purpose of a brand statement.

> *"You're not **defined** by your job title and you're not **confined** by your job description."* - Tom Peters

What makes a personal brand statement successful?

- o   Memorable
- o   Solution oriented
- o   Combines logic and emotion
- o   Describes your history in your career field
- o   Provides brand attributes that make you unique and valuable
- o   Gives specific examples
- o   Authentic

A personal brand statement is very similar to a brand statement for a product. Below is an example brand statement for a well-known retail store.

"We fulfill the needs and fuel the potential **(value)** of our guests **(audience)**. That means making Target your preferred shopping destination in all channels by delivering outstanding value, continuous innovation and exceptional experiences **(promise)**—consistently fulfilling our Expect More. Pay Less brand promise."

They described their **value** (what they are the best at), their **audience** (who they serve), and their **promise** (how they perform their value uniquely).

In the section below, is an example to show how these elements (value, audience and promise) come together to build a personal brand statement. (More personal brand statement examples on page 56).

Background: Jane is a CEO of a national furniture brand manufacturer and distributor.

AUDIENCE	PERSONA	PROMISE
New Clients	Sense of humor	Skilled at conflict resolution
	Hard worker	Ability to Unify Teams
	Positive	Identifying Problems
	Energetic	Managing Conflict
	Collaborative	
	Diplomatic	

PERSONAL BRAND STATEMENT

A focused and determined business leader, I offer the entrepreneurial stamina and wisdom to drive bottom line growth and lucrative business **(AUDIENCE)**, inspire employees to peak performance, and cultivate profitable business relationships built on respect, loyalty, and trust **(PERSONA)**. My easy-going sense of humor has been a defining management strategy to bring out the best in everyone, instill pride, and mobilize them to make their company the best in the industry **(PROMISE)**."

Jane's personal brand statement contains all the elements of a successful brand statement: it clearly tells you what Jane does, for whom and gives you an insight into how. *(Again, as you saw in the example for Target, this is identical to what marketers have to do for their products, which is to build a positioning statement for each product and its intended audience).*

Now it's your turn (fill out the box below):

1. Define your target **Audience** or ideal client base

2. Define a value statement by focusing your key attributes, or **Persona**

3. Define your positioning statement or **Promise**

4. Combine these elements to create a narrative that tells others about you!

In other words: Link your strongest attribute **(Persona)** and the results it created for someone **(Promise)** into a story.

AUDIENCE	PERSONA	PROMISE

PERSONAL BRAND STORY

> *"It's this simple: You are a brand. You are in charge of your brand. There is no single path to success. And there is no one right way to create the brand called You. Accept this: Start today. Or else."* -Tom Peters

EXAMPLE PERSONAL BRANDING STATEMENTS FOR INSPIRATION

- I help companies make the most of talent. I marry the sublime with the systematic — allowing for change with a focus on implementation. – **Business Consultant**

- I energize, focus and align manufacturing organizations, resulting in sustainable acceleration of processes, reduction in waste, and growth of profits. – **Consultant**

- I am a high-end service provider giving the sophisticated traveler a stylish and tailor-made experience at my Marrakech boutique hotel. – **Hotel Owner**

- Using my holistic insight and innovative Total Performance Scorecard principles, I promise to help my customers to realize their financial dreams. – **Financial Consultant**

- Inspirational CEO/CFO turned positive-psychologist resiliently transforming businesses and financial performance. – **Consultant**

- Inspire people to transform "stuck" career management plans to vibrant opportunity creating strategies. – **Career Coach**

- I love collaborating with forward-focused corporate leaders who know where they're going. – **Executive Coach**

- I use my quirky nature, confidence and passion for fun to motivate creative teams in ad agencies and marketing departments to work together more effectively to drive greater value for their organizations. – **Coach / Trainer**

  - A citizen of the world and a natural networker, I connect with senior leaders in all areas of the company (sales, marketing, R&D) and throughout all regions to deliver truly global marketing campaigns. I do this through constant collaboration and valuing of different ideas and insights. –**Marketing Consultant**

- With a passion for wine and a natural, open approach I inspire others to appreciate the pleasure of good wines in a fun way. – **Wine Tasting Host**

- Through my natural enthusiasm and my empathy for others, I inspire research and development professionals to develop innovative products in biotechnology. – **Biotech Manager**

- I use my 25 years of experience in – and passion for – marketing to help senior marketing executives in large organizations succeed by making marketing valued inside the organization. –**Marketing Trainer**

- Through my intuition and genuine concern for- and interest in – others, I build long-lasting, fruitful relationships with my team, my business partners and clients to drive consistent, recurring revenue for my company. – **Business Owner**

- [CEO Name Here] is defined as one of the most innovative and bottom line focused marketers and CEO's in the world. His string of dramatic firsts has followed every position he has held. His passion gives off a light that he carries wherever he goes. – **CEO**

- **Community Affairs Manager** with 10 years of experience visualizing, developing, and organizing company-wide philanthropic events, maintaining connections with hundreds of nonprofit organizations, coordinating diverse employee volunteer opportunities, and creating dynamic external and internal event communications.

- I help individuals and companies make the most of talent. I work as a part of the team. I am a straight shooter who isn't afraid to have the tough conversations. I also believe that people are more capable and valuable than they often give/get credit for. My method marries the sublime with the systematic — allowing for creativity and change with a strong focus on foundation and implementation. – Kristi Daeda (**Online branding and marketing**)

- As a **personal branding strategist** and cycling enthusiast, I combine my passion for bicycling and my drive for success to empower on-the-move careerists in global companies in Japan to believe, become, and be their brands. – Peter Sterlacci

- Through a unique combination of caring communication and collaboration, I inspire Fortune 500 professionals and executives not to leave their personalities at the door but to clearly communicate their unique value, raise their visibility by connecting with their true selves and successfully realize their career and personal goals. – Paul Copcutt

- **Career/Life Strategist**: I use my enthusiasm, forward thinking, and passion for self-direction to help clients identify their uniqueness and use it to take control of their careers and lives. – Walter Akana

- Helps thought leaders write great books in just 90 days. 300 satisfied clients so far… – Mindy Gibbins-Klein (**Author**)

References:

http://jorgensundberg.net/personal-brand-statement-examples-and-templates/ http://www.careerealism.com/personal-branding-statement-steps/#Ovx6VrYuYh34hkkl.99/

http://jorgensundberg.net/how-write-your-personal-brand-statement/ http://www.job-hunt.org/personal-branding/creating-your-personal-brand.shtml

PROMOTION

Objectives:
1. Tell Your Brand Story (start doing this by using your personal brand statement)
2. Develop Brand Ambassadors
3. Do you need a mentor?

Link your strongest attribute (**Persona**) and the results it created for someone (**Promise**) into a story.
Tell your story to one of your Brand Advocates (**Promotion**).

What are the ways you can tell your brand story?
- Business cards
- Resume/cover letter/reference documents
- Portfolio showcasing your work
- Present at Conferences
- Attend Conferences
- Volunteer
- One-on-one conversation
- Live it
- Blog
- LinkedIn
- Social media sites: Facebook, Twitter, etc.
- Articles
- Email signature
- Local Meet-up Interest Groups
- Networking events

Three things you can do today!
- Create, update or complete your LinkedIn profile --do you have a professional headshot? Use your brand statement as a way to introduce yourself to someone you just met. Update your LinkedIn profile summary with your brand statement.

- If you need a mentor, write 1-3 names of people you can call today and ask out for coffee!

- Send out a Personal Branding Assessment survey (example on page 60) to 10+ colleagues, friends or different networks, OR use The 360 Reach Personal Brand Assessment http://www.reachcc.com/360reach

RESOURCES – PERSONAL BRANDING ASSESSMENT SURVEY

PERSONAL BRANDING ASSESSMENT

Why is this important? Like all good product brand managers, first, we need to conduct some market research to help us understand the market, our intended target audience, what they think of the product, how they use it, how they describe it, etc. So, since you are now a brand manager of the brand YOU, you will also need to conduct market research on YOU. Below is a personal branding assessment, to be used as part of your assessment work of your persona and promise, that will help you to reconfirm or confirm how other people describe you, do they know who you are, and what you stand for.

I have my workshop participants conduct this survey in advance of the workshop, and they have found this to be an invaluable exercise. For example--the exercise has helped them to understand whether others also see their strengths as they do. For some, it has confirmed for them that they need to do some more work in the way of promoting their skills and value, since the results didn't match how they wanted to be described by their intended audience. For example—I had one participant tell me that her colleagues were describing her as "organized." Which is not a bad thing to be called, but, she wanted to be known for her leadership skills. So— this confirmed for her that she needed to be more strategic and find more opportunities to share her leadership skills with her intended audience.

- How to conduct the survey-- feel free to use an abbreviated version of this list of questions. Use one of the free online survey tools to gather and analyze the data. Each survey section below provides you with data that you can use to fill out the assessment (persona, promise and promotion) sections of the workbook.
- I recommend that you get at least 12 responses, from a variety of audiences (professional and personal networks). This is not necessarily a statistically valid survey pool, but, for this work, it's an informal survey, and we just want to get a general idea of whether how you describe who you are, and what you stand for is the same as how others describe and see you. Some survey results, and reviewing that information, will be better than not getting any data at all!
- Study the data, and find patterns in the responses. Some answers may be subjective, because some people will only have limited

experiences with you, so keep that in mind as you review the data, but nevertheless, it's a worthwhile exercise to reconfirm whether or not your brand is being seen how you wish others to see it.

Sample email invitation to participate in survey:
Dear <Name>: I'm working on a personal branding exercise and would value your candid input. Please answer the questions below (or insert survey link) as best you can. Short, bulleted answers are fine. I've included a sample list of Brand Attribute ideas to spark your thinking. Thank you for your help! Sincerely, <Your Name>

CORE VALUES

1. What do you think my core values are?

KEY STRENGTHS AND WEAKNESSES
1. What is my key skill set?
2. What is my expertise?
3. What are the weaknesses that may hold me back?

UNIQUE VALUE PROPOSITION
1. What is my unique expertise or value that differentiates me?

PERSONALITY/IMAGE ATTRIBUTES
1. How do I come across to others?
2. What are the key adjectives that describe my personality?
3. Describe my look and style.

LEADERSHIP ATTRIBUTES
1. What kind of a leader am I?

RELATIONSHIP ATTRIBUTES
1. What is it like to engage with me—professionally and socially?

WHAT IS A LIVING OR INANIMATE THING THAT BEST REPRESENTS MY BRAND? PLEASE EXPLAIN.

EXAMPLES:
A trusted Saint Bernard dog who always comes to the rescue

A Mini Cooper car that is efficient, fun to drive and has a quirky sense of style

The following list of potential brand attributes may help to spur ideas as you answer the questions above.

Sample Brand Attributes

Core Values	Strengths	Personality	Image
➤ Open mind	➤ Project Management	➤ Visionary	➤ Sophisticated
➤ Friendly	➤ People Management	➤ Positive	➤ Elegant
➤ Determination	➤ Financial or Operation	➤ Strategic	➤ Edgy
➤ Trust	Management	➤ Creative	➤ Classic
➤ Courage	➤ Technical Expertise	➤ Present	➤ Business casual
➤ Respect	➤ Strategic Planning	➤ Focused	➤ Urban
➤ Integrity	➤ Managing Conflict	➤ Flexible	➤ Artistic
➤ Passion	➤ Creative Problem Solving	➤ Inspirational	➤ Innovative
➤ Innovation	➤ Delivering Presentations	➤ Sense of humor	➤ Technology
➤ Transparency	➤ Decision Making	➤ Compassionate	savvy
➤ Adaptability	➤ Mentoring	➤ Patient	➤ Worldly
➤ Reliability	➤ Communication	➤ Results-oriented	➤ Cultured
➤ Accountability	➤ Strategic Vision	➤ Analytical	➤ Colorful
➤ Honesty	➤ Collaboration and	➤ Driven	➤ Conservative
➤ Giving back	Teamwork	➤ Passionate	➤ Academic
➤ Leadership	➤ Building and Leading	➤ Collaborative	➤ Professional
➤ Vision	Teams	➤ Personable	➤ Entrepreneurial
➤ Quality	➤ Leading Innovation	➤ Energetic	➤ Leader
➤ Diversity	➤ Streamlining Processes	➤ Friendly	➤ Hip
➤ Thought Leadership	➤ Striving for Results		
➤ Service	➤ Change Management		
➤ Helping Others	➤ Domain Expertise		
➤ Education			
➤ Competence			
➤ Responsibility			

ADDITIONAL RESOURCES

BOOKS
- Branding Pays, Karen Kang.
- BRAG! The Art of Tooting Your Own Horn without Blowing It. Peggy Klaus
- Lean In, Sheryl Sandberg

VIDEOS
- Personal Branding Guru, William Arruda
  http://www.youtube.com/watch?v=6paItEm2AF4
- Personal Branding: Four Principles of Career Distinction
- http://www.youtube.com/watch?v=iaFCmV5Ojqk&feature=related
- Branding and differentiation
  http://www.youtube.com/watch?v=8Py4XtVBImc&feature=related
- Personal Branding - What Color is Your Brand
- http://www.youtube.com/watch?v=XDohoPavchc&feature=related
- Five Myths About Personal Brands -
  http://www.youtube.com/watch?v=kKz2rmhhRzA

WEBSITES
- Tom Peters! http://tompeters.com/
- Branding Pays http://brandingpays.com/
- Smarter Networking http://www.smarter-networking.com/main/index.php Reach Personal Branding http://www.reachpersonalbranding.com/ Training, Coaching and Speaking Services, Pat O'Malley http://arrowleaf.net Catalyst, 2010. Advancing Latinas in the workplace: What managers need to know. Retrieved from http://www.catalyst.org/ This helpful site has several references for Latinas. The article discusses issues such as perceptions of leadership qualities, work-life balance, and interoffice communications.
- Dorie Clark, https://dorieclark.com/
- Eric Barker, https://www.bakadesuyo.com/about/ This site brings you science-based answers and expert insight on how to be awesome at life.

- Vanessa Van Edwards, https://www.scienceofpeople.com/ Level up your career and your relationships with the latest bite size human behavior science
- The Positioning Pioneers, https://www.ries.com/

ARTICLES
- "The Brand Called You", Tom Peters, http://www.fastcompany.com/28905/brand-called-you
- "Personal Branding 101," by Guisselle Nunez, Modern Latina, September 3, 2016, http://modernlatina.com/?p=8910
- Clark, D. (2014 Dec/Jan 2015). Personal Branding for the Image Impaired. More.com, 89-99, 17. new URL http://jamieprokell.com/Personal-Branding-for-the-Image-Impaired
- "Six Famous Entrepreneurs Who Show How Your Personal Brand Powers Deal Flow," https://www.entrepreneur.com/article/298599
- "Build a Personal Brand, Not Just a Career," https://www.forbes.com/sites/lisaquast/2012/11/19/build-a-personal-brand-not-just-a-career/#59f1c65a4e69

NOTES

ABOUT GUISSELLE NUÑEZ

Guisselle is focused on helping organizations and individuals achieve success through enduring marketing and personal branding strategies. Her passion for helping organizations communicate their value, combined with her 20 years of marketing and communications experience in various industries, enables her to provide guidance to her employers that is relevant, diverse, and results-oriented.

In her spare time, she volunteers as a mentor and serves on non-profit boards. She and her husband share a personal philosophy to "help improve the lives of others." She approaches her volunteer activities from the lens of her passion for marketing, and she tries to find opportunities to share those skills whenever possible—including sharing her knowledge and expertise on the importance of building your personal brand. She's also passionate about helping young Latinox with their personal and professional development.

Guisselle holds a Bachelor's Degree from Santa Clara University in History and Italian and a Master's Degree from Golden Gate University in Integrated Marketing Communications. She is adjunct faculty for the University of Phoenix, Silicon Valley Campus, and teaches undergraduate and graduate marketing courses. She conducts marketing and personal branding workshops to private and public sector clients. Born in Nicaragua, and raised in San Jose, CA, she is also fluent in Spanish.

Recognitions/Awards include:
- "Rookie Faculty of the Year," 2011, University of Phoenix, Bay Area Campus
- "Silicon Valley Women of Influence 2018," Silicon Valley Business Journal
- "Sisterhood Award 2018," Latina Coalition Silicon Valley

Follow on LinkedIn via: #takechargeofyourbrand
#personalbranding #brandyou #professionalwomen #branding #leanin

CONTACT AND BOOKINGS

For workshops, event hosting, and speaking events contact Guisselle directly via:

Email: guisselle@takechargeofyourbrand.com

Or fill out inquiry form: http://bit.ly/takechargeofyourbrand

Social: www.linkedin.com/in/guissellenunez

            @guissellevnunez

Share your story: Have you used personal branding to help you achieve your career dreams or other goals? Email me and share your story, and it may be featured in my next article!

Made in the USA
Monee, IL
03 January 2020